The Unabombe

of Ted Kaczyns..

By: Richard Miller

Ted Kaczynski brought terror

to the United States for nearly two

decades. He mailed and hand

delivered bombs that targeted

airplanes, universities,

businesses, and professors. He

manufactured homemade explosives and attempted to spark a revolution that rejected and fought against modernization and industrialization. It took the FBI seventeen years to finally catch him, and he gave up a promising career in academics to live a minimalistic life in the wilderness. Creating lengthy manifestos, papers, and essays, he questioned and rejected modern society. He went unsuspected for the 17 years he spent uncaught, and created widespread fear whenever anyone opened a package. He was eventually convicted of domestic terrorism, and his crimes still shake the fabric of American society.

Early Life

Kaczynski showed signs of being a genius even at an early age. He was born March 22, 1942 in Chicago, Illinois, to working class, Polish American, parents. He was a happy, easily to please child, until he experienced a severe case of hives. The ailment resulted in lengthy hospital stays, where he was isolated and denied human contact. When he was released, he showed signs of trauma and apathy. For months, he appeared completely emotionless and distant. Anytime he viewed photographs of when he was an infant, being held down by doctors examining his hives, he became overwhelmed, anxious, and disgruntled.

He exhibited heightened sympathy to caged animals, seemingly understanding the pain of forced captivity and isolation. After his family moved to Evergreen Park, Illinois, and he transferred schools, he was noted as becoming an engaged, social, and happy child. He took an IQ test, and scored a 167, indicating a genius-level IQ. Teachers and administrators decided to accelerate his education, and he skipped the sixth grade. He was unhappy with the decision, because he had developed meaningful friendships with his peers, and was considered a leader. When he was forced to interact with older kids, he was severely bullied, and went from

having a large group of good

friends to being a social pariah

and outcast.

He began exhibiting poor

social skills. He became

unresponsive in social situations

entirely, and couldn't handle

social pressure. His mother

became extremely concerned

with his social development, and

briefly considered signing him up for a study for autistic children.

When he entered high school, he excelled academically and joined a variety of groups, including the math, coin, German, and biology clubs. He also played the trombone in the school's band. Although he only had a small group of friends, they shared his interest in math and science. He was considered quiet and shy outside of this small group of friends.

Widely considered the most intelligent student in his high school, Kaczynski was deeply interested in math, and considered a brain. He took the most difficult classes the school offered, and received an accelerated education and course load. He ended up skipping the 11th grade too, and took summer classes so he could graduate when he was 15. Additionally, he was one of only five National Merit Scholars at his high school. He was accepted into Harvard, and offered a substantial scholarship, and so he moved to Boston and enrolled in the Ivy League school in 1958.

Harvard

When he arrived at Harvard, Kaczynski lived in a dorm structured towards the younger, more socially-unprepared students. He lived in a suite with several other students. For the remainder of his academic career, he lived in Eliot House. Classmates and dormmates noted that he mostly kept to himself, but was brilliant, friendly, polite, and extremely smart. He graduated in four years with a Bachelors of Arts in Mathematics.

While attending Harvard, Kaczynski signed up for a voluntary study ran by Harvard Psychology Professor Henry Murray. He was told that the study would consist of volunteers debating philosphy with other subjects, and that he would be writing essays on a variety of topics, including his own goals and beliefs.

However, the actual study consisted of the essays written by participants being given to an attorney, who would then verbally attack, insult, abuse, and demean the author. Kaczynski would be filmed while this brutal attack occurred, and the footage was repeatedly played back to him, with his reactions being noted and filmed. This occurred on a weekly basis for 3 years, and he devoted over 200 hours of his time participating in the study.

Graduate School

After graduating Harvard, Kaczynski applied to graduate

school in order to pursue a Masters and PhD in Mathematics. He was accepted to all three schools he applied to: The University of Michigan, University of California-Berkeley, and the University of Chicago.

He ultimately enrolled at the University of Michigan, even though it wasn't his first choice. The University of California-

Berkeley and the University of Chicago offered him no financial aid and also refused to offer him a teaching position. Conversely, the University of Michigan offered him a substantial grant and a guaranteed teaching position.

In 1962, he relocated to Ann Arbor and began his studies. He specialized in complex analysis, with a focus on geometric function theory. Professors were astounded by his drive and commitment to academics. Professor Peter Duran, when describing Kaczynski, stated "He was an unusual person. He was not like the other graduate students. He was much more focused about his work. He had a drive to discover mathematical truth."

Professors also claimed that describing him merely as "smart," was incredibly simplified and demeaning. Kaczynski was passionate about his studies and pursued his work to a higher goal than most of his peers. He graduated in 1967, receiving 12 As and 5 Bs. His dissertation, entitled "Boundary Functions," was universally praised. He won the University of Michigan's highly prestigious Sumner B. Myers Prize, which is awarded to the top mathematics dissertation.

The dissertation was widely considered an absolute masterpiece, and among the best written in the history of the University of Michigan. He followed up his dissertation with two journal articles before he left the University of Michigan, and later published three more.

Kaczynski, at the age of 25, became the youngest assistant mathematics professor in the history of the University of California Berkley in 1967. Although greatly respected by faculty, students expressed their dislike for his teaching methods and style. He was considered rigid, unapproachable, and off putting. He never answered questions and was known for teaching verbatim from textbooks.

In 1969, he unexpectedly resigned from teaching, and never gave the school a reason for leaving. Peers and colleagues suggested that, had he remained, he would have been promoted to a senior faculty position.

Colleagues also believe that the lack of advances in the field may have led to his departure. Most major innovations and theories in mathematics were proven in the 1960s, and there were few new frontiers left to study. The particular field of mathematics he had mastered was slowly becoming outdated and antiquated, and presently no longer exists, another reason he

may have resigned.

Montana

Kaczynski lived with his

parents in Lombard, Illinois for

two years after leaving the

University of California-Berkley.

He built a remote, primitive cabin

in the outskirts of Lincoln,

Montana, that didn't have any

electricity or running water. His goal was to become self-sufficient and live off the land, and to carve out a simple existence.

He frequently went to the local library, reading classics in their original languages. He worked odd jobs and rode a bicycle to and from town. He studied survivalist topics, from tracking game, to edible plants, and even organic farming.

His dream of a back to basics existence was shattered in 1975. When taking a hike to his favorite spot, he saw that it was now crowded and a road had been built through it. Tragically, this seemed to be the breaking point in his life, the moment when he decided to lash out at society.

He described this incident, stating that, "It's kind of rolling country, not flat, and when you get to the edge of it you find these ravines that cut very steeply in to cliff-like drop-offs and there was even a waterfall there. It was about a two days' hike from my cabin. That was the best spot until the summer of 1983. That summer there were too many people around my cabin so I decided I needed some peace. I went back to the plateau and when I got there I found they had put a road right through the middle of it ... You just can't imagine how upset I was. It was from that point on I decided that, rather than trying to acquire further wilderness skills, I would work on getting back at the

system. Revenge."

He decided to fight the self-coined industrial-technology complex. He targeted local real estate developers, and sought to undermine, sabotage, and destroy their ability to complete their projects. For the first time, he devoured books on topics covering sociology and political philosphy. His new goal was to ignite a revolution against industrialization and technological innovation. When describing his new objective in life, he stated that, "As I see it, I don't think there is any controlled or planned way in which we can dismantle the industrial system. I think that the only way we will get rid of it is if it breaks down and collapses ...

The big problem is that people don't believe a revolution is possible, and it is not possible precisely because they do not believe it is possible. To a large extent I think the eco-anarchist movement is accomplishing a great deal, but I think they could do it better ... The real revolutionaries should separate themselves from the reformers ...

And I think that it would be good if a conscious effort was being made to get as many people as possible introduced to the wilderness. In a general way, I think what has to be done is not to try and convince or persuade the majority of people that we are right, as much as try to increase tensions in society to the point where things start to break down.

To create a situation where people get uncomfortable enough that they're going to rebel. So the question is, how do you increase those tensions?"

The bitter Montana experience seemingly pushed Kaczynski over the edge, and he decided to use his intellect and abilities to attack and harm those he blamed for creating the society

he hated.

The Bombings

He decided to build bombs,

and target those who were

considered adversarial to his

objectives and goals. His first

bomb targeted Buckley Crist, who

was a mechanical engineering

professor at Northwestern

University. Kaczynski dropped the package off in a parking lot at the University of Chicago. The package arrived to Crist after it was returned to sender.

Suspicious, because Crist had never mailed the package to the original recipient, he wisely called campus security. The security officer opened the box. The bomb exploded, but only left a minor wound on the security guard's left hand.

The first bomb Kaczynski constructed was inferior, poorly designed, and largely ineffective. He used hand crafted wooden ends on the pipe bombs instead of metal, which resulted in a minimally impactful blast, because wooden ends don't possess the necessary strength to allow the bomb to build up the pressure it needs in the pipe. He used a rubber band to fasten tension a nail to construct the trigger, which led to six matches lighting to ignite the power.

Kaczynski later upgraded his bombs to increase their lethality, using batteries and more refined powders.

After the bombing, he briefly worked with his younger brother and father at a foam rubber factory back in Illinois. The job lasted for three months - he began in May 1978, and was fired by his own brother in August. Kaczynski allegedly wrote demeaning, offensive limericks about a female employee, and posted them at work.

His next target was chosen, and attacked, in 1979. Kaczynski decided to construct a homemade explosive, and place it in the cargo hold of American Airlines Flight 444. The plane was a Boeing 727, and was completing a trip from Chicago to Washington D.C. The bomb malfunctioned, and failed to ignite. It did begin smoking, and the plane made an

emergency landing.

The FBI began investigating

the incident. They concluded the

bomb, had it successfully gone

off, could have easily blown up

the entire plane. They named the

case UNABOM. The FBI created

a force in conjunction with the

ATF and U.S. Postal Service in

1979, and began devoting

significant time and resources

looking into the victims. The

research proved to be useless, as

no correlation or relationship

could be found to connect the

victims, preventing a potential

suspect from being identified.

The victims seemed random,

and, in 1980, the FBI's Behavioral

Sciences Unit released a detailed

profile on the suspect behind the

attempted bombing. Their

summation was that the suspect

was intelligent, and likely had

connections to scholars or

academia. Additionally, the

suspect likely had received a

formal, advanced education, and

obtained a degree in a science

field.

In 1983, the psychosocial

profile completed by the

Behavioral Sciences Unit was dismissed as inaccurate and unhelpful. The FBI instead supported an alternate theory which hypothesized that the suspect was a blue collar, low level airline mechanic.

The task force offered a $1 million reward for any information that led to the identification, arrest, and conviction of the suspect.

In 1980, he mailed a bomb in a package to Percy Wood, who was the President of United Airlines. Wood sustained minor injuries, including cuts and burns on most of his body, but made a full recovery.

He sent a bomb to the University of Utah in 1981, but it was defused before it could detonate.

On May 5, 1982, Janet Smith, a secretary at Vanderbilt University, opened a package containing a bomb and suffered severe burns on her hands, and shrapnel became lodged in parts of her body.

Less than a month later, on June 2, 1982, Diogenes Angelakos, an engineering professor at the University of California-Berkeley, Kaczynski's old employer, suffered severe burns and had shrapnel lodged in his hands and face.

The first permanent injuries suffered by one of Kaczynski's victims happened on May 15,

1985, when John Hauser, a graduate student at the University of California-Berkeley, lost four fingers, sustained a severed artery in his right arm, and suffered permanent, partial vision loss in both of his eyes.

On June 13, 1985, a bomb sent to Boeing was successfully defused before exploding.

On November 15, 1985, professor of psychology James McConnell suffered temporary hearing loss, and research assistant Niklaus Suino received serious burns and shrapnel wounds when they opened a package with one of Kaczynski's bombs. Both worked at the University of Michigan.

The next victim was the first fatality of Kaczynski's, when on December 11, 1985, Hugh Scrutton, the owner of a computer store in Sacramento, California died while opening a package sent by Kaczynski.

Kaczynski stayed quite for nearly 7 years, until his next victim, geneticist Charles

Epsteitn, lost 3 fingers and suffered irreversible hearing loss.

Two days later, on June 24, 1993, David Gelernter, a professor of computer science at Yale University, lost his right hand and was severely burned by Kaczynski's bomb.

Kaczynski's second fatality occurred on December 10, 1994,

when advertising executive Thomas Moser died while opening a package containing a homemade bomb.

Kaczynski's final attack, and last fatality, happened on April 24, 1995. The victim, Gilbert Murray, was a timber industry lobbyist.

Most of the bombs used were delivered by the post office to the unknowing victims.

The Unabomber Manifesto

Kaczynski boldly demanded in 1995 that his personal, 35,000-page manifesto, which he entitled "Industrial Society and Its Future," be published in a reputable publication with access to the

public at large.

He mailed letters to a

multitude of media outlets,

proclaiming that if a respectable

publication ran his essay, he

would "desist from terrorism," and

stop his attacks.

Although controversy ensued

about whether it was beneficial to

publish the piece, Attorney General Janet Reno and FBI Director Louise Freeh believed it would protect public safety if the manifesto was published. Originally, the Penthouse offered to print the work, but Kaczynski responded by demanding that a more "respectable" publication run it, or his attacks would resume.

Eventually, the Washington Post and the New York Times published the "Unabomber Manifesto" on September 19, 1995.

Kaczynski wrote the manifesto with a typewriter, and consistently used "we" and "FC (Freedom Club)." Additionally, to emphasize words and phrases, he used capitalization, because typewriters lacked the ability to italicize or underline words.

In his manifesto, Kaczynski warned people about the consequences of technology. He voiced concerns that technological advancements had led to decreased and diminished human interaction, people dedicating their lives to unworthy goals, and had caused suffering.

He warned about advances to genetics, which, he argued, would lead to genetic engineering that would be used to take away people's free will. Kaczynski believed that eugenics would lead to a society where people are manufactured, and, like cars, are built based on the wants and needs of society,

This focus on genetics would result in the essence of humans dying. He argued that industrial society would cause human suppression, because industrialization wants people to be controlled, and to refuse to exercise their freedom. Without control, Kaczynski argued, the industrial system will fail. He warned that the system was working on controlling human behavior, and, left unopposed, the system would successfully obtain full control over human behavior within 40-100 years.

He believed that this objective would be accomplished unless people fight back and resist, and begin to reject technology.

The essay, dubbed the "Unabomber Manifesto," was widely praised by academics, journalists, and intellectuals. It was described as logical, thoughtful, convincing, and artfully written. Readers never doubted the author's sanity or intelligence.

The Investigation

Despite a $1 million reward, investigators had few promising leads. Most research led to dead ends. The general belief was that the suspect was from the Chicago area, had connections to Salt Lake City, and an association with San Francisco.

They failed to find any forensic evidence, or any connections between the targets.

Publishing the "Unabomber Manifesto" likely was the reason why Kaczynski was investigated, and ultimately arrested and convicted. After the manifesto was published, the FBI received thousands of tips, and received multiple letters purported to be written by the Unabomber. While investigators carefully reviewed every tip, as unlikely or preposterous as they sounded, Kaczynski's own brother began suspecting Kaczynski was responsible.

David Kaczynski, Ted's younger brother, had started to consider that his brother was the Unabomber. The brothers became estranged in 1990, and last saw each other in person in 1985. David had moved on, married, and started a family. His wife begged David to read the Unabomber Manifesto, believing that the document proved her brother-in-law was the wanted domestic terrorist. David started reviewing old letters to the editor Ted had submitted to newspapers and other media outlets in the 1970s, in which he railed against environmental destruction.

David took his wife's advice, and covertly hired a private investigator, Susan Swanson, to discreetly and quietly follow Ted. David asked Susan to keep tabs on Ted's day to day life, his activities, and his whereabouts. David also hired Tony Bisceglie, an attorney from Washington D.C., to compile the results of Swanson's sleuthing, and prepare to present it to the FBI. David also wanted to ensure the FBI would not raid Ted's home, because recent stings had resulted in casualties, and David felt Ted may react violently to such a confrontation.

Biscelglie contacted former FBI criminal profiler Clinton Van Zandt in 1996, asking him to compare letters David had that were written by Ted, to the

Unabomber Manifesto. Van Zandt

had two separate analytics team

compare the writings. The first

review concluded there was a

60% chance that the same

person had authored the

Unabomber Manifesto and the

letters. The second set of

analyses found that the chances

exceeded 60%, and

recommended that Biscelglie

contact the FBI and inform them

of the findings. Shortly after,

Biscelgie submitted an essay Ted

Kaczynski wrote in 1971 to the

FBI. The UNABOM task force

concluded that the essay and

Unabomber Manifesto were

authored by the same person,

and Ted Kaczynski's background

and life situation matched the

suspect's profile.

Although David attempted to

stay anonymous, the FBI soon

validated the information that

came from him, and immediately

interviewed him and his wife in

the presence of their attorney.

David continued to supply the

investigators with additional

letters, some with the original

envelopes, which greatly aided the FBI in developing an accurate timeline of Ted Kaczynski's life and crimes.

David worked with the task force diligently for several months. In April 1996, his identity as the person who came forward to the FBI about the Unabomber case was leaked to CBS. Fortunately, Dan Rather, a CBS anchorman, called Louis Freeh to inform him of the leak, to ensure that the Unabomber was taken down. Rather gave Freeh 24 hours to execute a search and arrest warrant. The FBI successfully obtained the appropriate warrants from a federal judge in Montana, and executed warrants at Ted Kaczynski's Montana cabin. They briefly placed Kaczynski's old high school on lock down while retrieving his old school records.

Capture

On April 3, 1996, Ted Kaczynski was arrested in his remote Montana cabin. He was found unbathed and unkept. FBI agents found ingredients to make bombs, more than 40,000 hand written journals containing bomb making recipes and experiments, printouts of articles involving Unabomber crimes, and a live explosive prepared for mailing. There was also a typed manuscript, "Industrial Society and Its Future," found in Kaczynski's cabin. The arrest concluded the most costly, expensive, and extensive FBI investigation in American history.

Plea Agreement

Kaczynski was indicted on ten counts of illegally transporting, mailing, and using bombs, and three counts of murder in April 1996. Kaczynski was initially represented by two federal public defenders, Judy Clarke and Michael Donahoe. Both planned to raise the argument that Kaczynski was mentally unfit, and wanted to enter a Not Guilty by Reason of Insanity plea.

Kaczynski fired his attorneys, and refused to claim insanity.

Kaczynski hired attorney Tony Serro, who agreed not to enter an insanity plea, but the court did not allow the request to go through.

Kaczynski attempted suicide on January 9, 1998, by trying to hang himself with his underwear. It was unsuccessful, and he was placed in a monitored cell on suicide watch. He had visible marks around his neck when he appeared in court the following day.

Throughout the pre-trial process, several physiatrists diagnosed Kaczynski with schizophrenia and similar conditions. Kaczynski continued to deny he had any mental issues.

He was declared fit to stand trial on January 21, 1998, and entered a guilty plea on all counts the following day, avoiding the death penalty. He was sentenced to life imprisonment in a federal detention facility, and was ineligible for parole. He appealed the sentence, claiming the plea was entered involuntarily, but the appeal was denied.

Prison

Kaczynski is currently incarcerated at the ADX Florence,

a super max security prison in

Florence, Colorado. While

incarcerated, he befriended

Timothy McVeigh and Ramzi

Yousef. His cabin was taken by

the government, and all of its

contents were sold in order to pay

restitution to Kaczynski's victims.

The university of Michigan

has over 400 letters written by

Kaczynski on display in its special

collections. All of the letters have been written after his arrest.

The Kaczynski Family

Kaczynski's family has, likewise, been torn apart by Ted's actions as the Unabomber. David felt ashamed at turning in his brother. When he told their mother, he expected a bad reaction. Instead, his mother kissed David on the forehead, and said he did the right thing.

In 1969, Ted and David spent a joyous summer together, traversing Canada in search of a plot of land where Ted could begin his new, survivalist life. They camped out in Nebraska on the way back home. They even bought a plot of land together, and built their own cabin.

Ted's relationship with his parents and brother began deteriorating in the mid-1970s. In 1977, during a tyrannical letter to his parents, Ted accused his parents of never having loved him. David mailed Ted a letter in 1989, stating that he was abandoning his cabin in the wilderness in Texas, and moving to New York after he fell in love.

Ted didn't take the news well. He wrote a scathing, belittling 20-page letter to David, deriding his decision. Lambasting his selfishness, he stated that David lacked integrity, morality, and refused to live a pure life.

David and Ted never talked again. Ted told David at the end of the letter that he no longer wanted a relationship with his younger brother. He told David to never call or write him again, and to cut off all communication. Ted even went so far as to instruct David that, if there was a severe emergency, that he was to write a line underneath the stamp of a letter. If the letter didn't have that line, he would burn the letter without opening it. If David abused the rule, Ted would forever end all communication.

David only wrote Ted one more letter, and it included the specially requested line. He wrote to tell Ted that their father was diagnosed with lung cancer, and was dying. Ted sent a response thanking David for the information, but Ted mentioned nothing else, and never saw his father.

David wrestled with the decision to turn Ted in. He felt horrible simply considering betraying his brother, and feared Ted would be executed. Making matters worse, David's mother always told him to never abandon family, and to never turn his back on his brother.

The FBI told David that, in exchange for his cooperation, they would not seek the death penalty against Ted. They broke their promise, and David feared he would be responsible for Ted's execution.

David has published a book, entitled "Every Last Tie," addressing his brother's mental illness. In 2016, Ted began writing letters to multiple news outlets, stating he wanted to grant an interview. Ted requested that anyone interested in conducting an interview describe themselves, explain why they should be trusted, and affirm that he doesn't suffer from any mental health

conditions.

David has worked advocating

against the death penalty,

motivated by what he felt was a

betrayal by federal prosecutors

when they sought the death

penalty against his brother. He

received the $1 million reward in

the Unabomber case, and

decided to donate it to the victims of his brother.

Ted sought a means to dispel David's accusations that Ted suffers from severe mental health issues. Ted wrote a letter to multiple media outlets that stated the following: ""...I am ready to speak to someone from the media regarding my brother's recent comments and to discuss how they are being used to torment me."

Kaczynski lists his conditions for granting an interview, including, "tell me who you are," "why I should trust you," and "[affirm] that you understand that I am NOT mentally ill."" None accepted Ted's request.

David continues to write to his brother, and sends him Christmas cards every year. Ted refuses to write back, or speak to David.

When Ted was told that David was the person who reported him to the FBI, he stated, "That's impossible. David loves me. He'd never do that."

Legacy

It stands to reason that, had Ted Kaczynski not submitted his "Unabomber Manifesto," he never would have been caught. Shockingly, he never left even a shred of incriminating evidence. The FBI hit a dead end during their Unabomber investigation, and the only thing that broke the case was Kaczynski's Manifesto.

The only valid tip that led to his arrest was from his brother, who kept and stockpiled nearly every letter Ted ever wrote him.

Nobody ever saw Kaczynski as a threat, and never saw any indications of violence. People were shocked that he was the Unabomber, and even his Manifesto is held in high regard.

Multiple prestigious scholars and academics have praised the 35,000-word document as a masterpiece.

The only person who knew Kaczynski that vehemently believes he is mentally ill is his brother.

The FBI sketches were also highly inaccurate. Their profile was, at times, shockingly wrong. Kaczynski built all of his bombs from scrap material, which made them impossible for the FBI to trace. His off the grid lifestyle made it equally challenging to investigate him, and because he lived in such a remote area and was rarely seen in public, he was

never considered a suspect until
David Kaczynski intervened with
the investigation. David, in fact,
never would have reported his
suspicions to the FBI without his
wife's urging.

Kaczynski's former cabin has
been turned into a museum. The
land he owned in Montana, a total
of 1.4 acres, was originally listed

for sale at $154,500.00. The Montana real estate company selling the home was criticized for advertising it with the tagline ""Own a Piece of U.S. History: Home of the Unabomber." Most land of similar size sells for no more than $50,000. On top of that, the property did not include the cabin.

Kaczynski was furious when the government ordered his property to be sold for restitution. They even sold parts of his writings and journals, leading Kaczynski to sue over first amendment rights. He claimed that selling uncompleted works violated his right to free speech, but he was unsuccessful and the works were quickly sold.

Kaczynski staunchly advocates for an accurate portrait of his life. He regularly writes to members of the media, and has shared his thoughts about documentaries and books released about his crimes. He denied that the Murray study he participated in while at Harvard was traumatic, or as bad as people claim, stating that the study as a whole was wildly

exaggerated.

In 2010, he published a book,

entitled "Anti-Tech Revolution:

Why and How." The book

received mostly favorable

reviews, and discusses how

environmental movements have

largely failed, warning that

technology will likely destroy

society. He posits a plan to prevent all of this destruction, advocating for new approaches, and the book is described as a determinist philosphy argument.

The case was ultimately solved because of forensic linguistics. Because there was no physical evidence, FBI specialists poured over tens of thousands of pages

and painstakingly compared the
word choice, writing style,
themes, and idiosyncrasies to
determine if Kaczynski was the
Unabomber. They could find
minor tidbits of biographical
details that helped them build an
initial profile, and then conclude
Ted Kaczynski was the
Unabomber. The FBI relied more
on forensic linguists in the

Unabomber case than ever before, and the field is now viewed with newfound importance.

CPSIA information can be obtained
at www.ICGtesting.com
Printed in the USA
LVHW052340160623
749989LV00002B/268

9 781721 837151